The Ultimate Bento Box Cookbook

New and Exciting Lunches Your Kids Will Love!

BY: SOPHIA FREEMAN

Liability

This publication is meant as an informational tool. The individual purchaser accepts all liability if damages occur because of following the directions or guidelines set out in this publication. The Author bears no responsibility for reparations caused by the misuse or misinterpretation of the content.

Copyright

Table of Contents

Introduction

When I was a kid, lunches consisted of plain brown paper bags stuffed with a soggy sandwich, usually a piece of fruit of some kind and a treat if we were lucky. Nowadays, there are so many creative ways to pack lunches for your little guys and bento boxes are the newest craze in lunch boxes. What I love about my bento box is that it is collapsible at the bottom, so I can flatten it down to save space if I need to. The collapsible bottom also means that there is more space for extra treats like yogurt drinks or cookies.

Most boxes have a gel filled liquid inside a container that are frozen and keeps the food chilled all day. I will pop that container into the freezer at night and it is good to go by the next morning.

1. Southwestern Pasta Salad

Wholly Guacamole makes a delicious single serving guacamole cup that I like to use in my kids' lunches. There are also many single serving yogurt cups you can use instead of the Greek yogurt.

Preparation time-15 minutes

Servings-8

Ingredients

- 12 ounces whole wheat mini shells, cooked and drained
- 15 ounces drained can black beans, rinsed
- 15 ounces drained can corn, rinsed
- 8 ounces cherry tomatoes quartered
- 6 diced mini sweet peppers,
- 1 thinly sliced green onion
- 4 ounces lowfat Cheddar cheese, shredded
- 4 ounces creamy Ranch dressing
- 1 ounce blue tortilla chips
- 1 ounce single serving mini guacamole containers
- 4 ounces Greek yogurt
- 1/2 sliced banana
- ½ ounce granola

Directions

1. When pasta has cooled, mix in with black beans, corn, sweet peppers, green onion, cheddar cheese and Ranch dressing in a large mixing bowl.

2. In separate compartments in the bento box, add blue tortilla chips, guacamole, yogurt, banana and granola.

2.Mac N' Cheese Muffins

These treats are simple to make and perfectly proportioned for a bento box. I would suggest packing apple slices and some crackers to go with the cheesy goodness.

Preparation time-5 minutes

Servings-12

Ingredients

- 8 ounces baby cut carrots
- 8 ounces broccoli florets
- 3/4 sweet onion
- 8 ounces Cheddar cheese, shredded
- 8 ounces shredded mozzarella cheese
- 1 egg
- ½ ounce room-temperature butter, unsalted
- 1/3 ounce olive oil
- 14 ½ ounces cooked whole-wheat macaroni noodles
- 8 ounces whole-wheat breadcrumbs, divided

Directions

1. Preheat oven to 350 degrees Fahrenheit. Coat a 12-cup muffin tin with cooking spray.

2. Place carrots, onion and broccoli in a blender and puree until smooth

3. In a large mixing bowl, combine cheddar cheese, mozzarella cheese, egg, unsalted butter and olive oil until just mixed.

4. Add cooked macaroni, carrot puree mixture and 4 ounces of bread crumbs to the cheese mixture. Stir until just incorporated.

5. Spoon even amounts into the prepared muffin tin and sprinkle the rest of the bread crumbs on top.

6. Bake for 30 minutes until golden brown.

3.Homemade Lunchables

If you have a bento box with lots of little containers then this is a simple and delicious lunch to pack for school. There are also many inexpensive small containers at the dollar store you can buy for this kind of lunch.

Preparation time-10 minutes

Servings-1

Ingredients

- 1 ounce sliced turkey breast, rolled and halved
- 1 slice low-fat Cheddar cheese, quartered
- 1 hardboiled egg
- 4 whole-wheat crackers
- 4 ounces green grapes, seedless
- 1 ounce pretzel sticks
- 2 ounces single serving mini guacamole containers

Directions

Place all Ingredients separately in the bento box using separate containers. You can use paper liners to avoid food getting soggy.

4.Simple Picnic Bento

This delicious yogurt-based picnic lunch makes my kids laugh every time. I will sometimes add small M&Ms or chocolate chips on the raisins to make it look like the ants are carrying baby ants.

Preparation time-15 minutes

Servings-6

Ingredients

- 3 ounces plain Greek yogurt
- ½ ounce honey
- 1/3 ounce Dijon mustard
- 1/4 teaspoon salt
- 1/4 teaspoon pepper
- 1/4 teaspoon garlic powder
- 16 ounces shredded rotisserie chicken
- 5 ½ ounces red grapes, seedless
- 1 ounce green onions, chopped
- 2 ounces pecans, chopped
- 1 stalk celery, cut into 1/3rds
- 15 raisins
- 1 ounce natural peanut butter
- 8 whole-wheat crackers
- 4 ounces strawberries, halved

Directions

1. In a large mixing bowl, combine Greek yogurt, honey, Dijon, garlic powder, salt and pepper until mixed well.

2. Mix in shredded chicken, chopped pecans and green onions.

3. Place peanut butter in the celery and add raisins to make it look like ants

4. Pack the yogurt mixture with crackers and sliced strawberries

5.Caprese Zoodle Salad

This salad is a simple and refreshing lunch your kids will enjoy again and again. I like to pack some freeze-dried fruit and crackers with this salad to make a complete meal.

Preparation time-15 minutes

Servings-4

Ingredients

- 1 1/2 ounces olive oil
- 1 teaspoon honey
- ¼ ounce balsamic vinegar
- 2 medium zucchini
- 16 ounces cherry tomatoes, cut in half
- 8 ounces small mozzarella balls
- 2 ½ ounces chopped basil

Directions

1. In a small mixing bowl, whisk olive oil, vinegar and honey until combined

2. Cut zucchini into spirals with a potato peeler and transfer to a bowl.

3. Mix in tomatoes, cheese and basil until fully combined. Toss salad in balsamic dressing

6.5-Ingredient Broccoli Grape Salad

I find broccoli very tough when it is raw so I will soak it for a bit in cold water to soften it a bit. Pat the broccoli dry with a paper towel until dry before adding it to the rest of the **Ingredients**.

Preparation time-15 minutes

Servings-8

Ingredients

- 16 ounces broccoli florets, broken into small pieces
- 8 ounces red seedless grapes, cut in half
- 3 ounces Cheddar cheese, shredded
- 2 ounces red onion, chopped
- 2 ounces bacon ranch salad dressing

Directions

1. Combine all Ingredients in a large mixing bowl.

2. Store in the refrigerator for 35 minutes before adding to lunch box.

7.Brown Bear Bento Box with Fruit Salad

This adorable and colorful bento box will delight your kids at lunchtime. Some ideas for colorful fruit are pineapple, raspberries, blackberries and light green grapes.

Preparation time-5 minutes

Servings-1

Ingredients

- ½ ounce soy butter
- 3 graham cracker squares
- 9 blueberries
- 1/2 banana, sliced into thirds
- 8 ounces assorted fruit chopped
- 3 sliced mini sweet peppers
- ½ ounce Ranch dressing

Directions

1. Spread graham crackers with butter and top with banana and blueberries in the shape of eyes and noses

2. Arrange the colorful fruit in one of the other containers to create a rainbow salad

3. Pack the sweet peppers and Ranch dressing to complete the lunch box

8. Butterfly Bento Box

This bento box will make your little one smile when they see the butterfly looking up at them at lunchtime. You can add different types of vegetables and fruit to the rest of the box.

Preparation time-15 minutes

Servings-1

Ingredients

- 2 slices whole-wheat bread
- 1 ounce natural peanut butter
- 1 teaspoon honey
- 1/2 small thinly sliced banana
- 1 clementine
- 2 ounces pomegranate arils
- ½ ounce chocolate chips
- 4 ounces cucumbers, sliced

Directions

1. Spread each slice of whole-wheat bread with natural peanut butter

2. Top with banana slices and honey and close sandwich. Cut the sandwich with a butterfly shaped cookie cutter.

3. Arrange the rest of the Ingredients together or separate in the other containers.

9.Easy Turkey Wrap

This simple wrap tastes great and is a quick fix when you run out of bread! I have added pickle slices to this wrap as well for a unique flavour.

Preparation time-15 minutes

Servings-4

Ingredients

- 8 ounces thickly-sliced turkey, low-sodium
- 4 slices provolone cheese
- ½ ounce light Ranch dressing
- 4 ounces peeled carrots, thinly sliced
- 1 sliced tomato
- 8 ounces lettuce, shredded
- 1/2 thinly sliced cucumber
- 1 seeded and sliced red bell pepper
- 1 peeled and pitted avocado, mashed with a fork

Directions

1. Arrange turkey slices flat on a cutting board and top with 1 cheese slice each

2. Spread even amounts of the dressing on each cheese slice. Evenly divide the rest of the Ingredients on the dressing.

3. Roll the turkey around the filling and secure with a toothpick

10.Sandwich Kabobs

Some sides that go well with these kabobs include sliced apple, Greek yogurt or freeze-dried fruit packs. I also like to add small sour pickles to the ends for that delicious taste.

Preparation time-20 minutes

Servings-1

Ingredients

- Beet Chips
- 1 large peeled beet, thinly sliced
- 1/2 teaspoon sea salt
- 1 teaspoon olive oil
- Sandwich Kabobs
- 4 grape tomatoes, halved
- 4 cubes Cheddar cheese, lowfat
- 2 slices whole wheat bread, quartered
- 2 slices halved ham, low-sodium
- 1/2 sliced small cucumber, cut lengthwise in 4 ribbons

Directions

1. Preheat oven to 375 degrees Fahrenheit. Line a baking sheet with parchment paper

2. Arrange sliced beets on the baking sheet and brush with olive oil. Season with sea salt.

3. Bake beets for 25 minutes until edges brown. Remove from heat and cool for 5-10 minutes

4. Place beets on parchment-lined baking sheet, brush with oil and sprinkle with salt.

5. Bake 20 minutes or until edges start to brown. Remove from oven and let cool.

6. Using mini skewers, assemble the kabob with the Ingredients in any order you desire

7. Pack kabobs with beet chips and sides

11.Nacho Lunchbox

Bring one of your kids' favourite dishes to the lunchbox with this simple nacho bento box recipe. I like to add some cheese sticks to this recipe as well as a bit of salsa for flavour.

Preparation time-10 minutes

Servings-1

Ingredients

- 1 ounce scoop tortilla chips, multigrain
- 2 ounces drained and rinsed black beans, low-sodium
- 2 ounces iceberg lettuce shredded
- 1 ounce Tex Mex cheese, shredded
- 6 small tomatoes, cut in half
- 1 ounce Wholly Guacamole mini
- 1 small apple

Directions

In separate small containers, arrange Ingredients separately to be ready to assemble for lunch

12.Cheese and Bean Quesadilla

Pack this lunch with some sliced apples, guacamole and salsa. You might want to wrap the tortilla in tin foil and place in a lined lunchbox to keep it warm.

Preparation time-10 minutes

Servings-1

Ingredients

- 1 (10") whole wheat tortilla
- 4 ounces drained and rinsed white beans, smashed
- 2 ounces Mexican cheese, shredded
- 1 small sliced apple
- 2-ounce Wholly Guacamole® mini

Directions

1. Heat frying pan on medium heat

2. Spread beans on whole-wheat tortilla and top wit shredded cheese.

3. Fold tortilla in half and cook in the frying pan for 2-3 minutes per side until crispy and cheese has melted.

4. Remove tortilla from heat and cut in 4 pieces

13.Sandwich Bento Box

Skewers are a fun and simple way of packing a variety of foods in the bento box without taking up too much space. If you don't have sandwich rounds available, then use whole bread.

Preparation time-10 minutes

Servings-1

Ingredients

- 1 whole-wheat Nature's Own sandwich round
- 1 slice turkey, low-sodium
- 1 slice low-fat Cheddar cheese
- 4 mini skewers
- 1 slice pineapple, cut into 8 pieces
- 8 blueberries
- 8 mini marshmallows
- 4 slices cucumber
- 4 cherry tomatoes

Directions

1. Assemble sandwich with turkey and cheese.

2. Assemble skewers by threading pineapple, blueberries and marshmallow.

3. Pack cucumber and tomatoes in another container in the bento box

14. Vegetable Caesar Pasta Salad

Serve this pasta salad with some freeze-dried fruit like the kind produced by Crispy Green. Mandarin orange segments and cheese sticks are also excellent sides.

Preparation time-15 minutes

Servings-6

Ingredients

- 12 ounces cooked bowtie pasta
- 8 ounces fresh spinach, chopped
- 15-ounce drained and rinsed can low-sodium chickpeas
- 4 ounce mini sweet peppers, sliced
- 4 ounces cherry tomatoes, halved
- 2 ounces Caesar dressing
- ½ ounce Parmesan cheese, grated

Directions

1. Mix all **Ingredients** in a large mixing bowl and transfer to the large container of the bento box

15.Orzo Bento Salad

This salad is healthy and filling. I usually pack this with some crackers, sliced fruit and yogurt for a complete lunch.

Preparation time-15 minutes

Servings-4

Ingredients

- 6 ounces cooked orzo, drained, not rinsed
- 6 ounces chopped broccoli florets
- 3 ounces yellow cherry tomatoes, cut in half
- 3 ounces red cherry tomatoes, cut in half
- 5 ½ ounces drained and rinsed garbanzo beans, low-sodium
- 2 chopped sprigs basil
- 2 ounces Parmesan cheese, grated
- 1 ounce olive oil and vinegar salad dressing

Directions

1. Pour cooked orzo into large serving bowl.

2. Place ice cubes in a bowl full of water to make an ice back for the broccoli

3. Place broccoli in a microwave-safe dish with a cover with ½ ounce of water. Cook on high for 30 seconds.

4. Drain broccoli and place in the ice bath. Drain well and add broccoli to the cooked orzo.

5. Add the rest of the Ingredients and toss to combine

16.Turkey Sushi

If you are like me, the word sushi fills you with anxiety when preceded by the word 'homemade'. This is a sushi recipe I have ready many times and it is super easy to make!

Preparation time-15 minutes

Servings-2

Ingredients

- 9" spinach tortilla
- 1 ounce light Ranch dressing
- 3 slices low-fat deli turkey breast
- 4 ounces rice, cooked
- 2 ounces carrots, grated
- 2 peeled slices seedless cucumber, cut into strips
- 2 ounces lettuce, shredded
- 1 thinly sliced piece tomato, cut into strips
- 1 thinly sliced piece low-fat Cheddar cheese, cut into strips

Directions

1. Place tortilla on a microwave-safe plate and heat for 15 seconds on high

2. Remove tortilla and spread with dressing. Top with a turkey and add cooked rice to one half of the tortilla.

3. In a line on top of the tortilla, arrange the rest of the Ingredients.

4. Roll the tortilla around the filling and cut into 2" slices.

17. Vegan Greek Pita

Not all kids are into onions and garlic, but if you are lucky to have one who is, then this is the recipe for you. You might want to pack some mints too, so they don't drive their classmates away.

Preparation time-15 minutes

Servings-3

Ingredients

- ½ ounce olive oil
- 1 chopped sweet onion
- 1 chopped red bell pepper
- ¾ ounce oregano
- 3 minced cloves garlic
- 3 whole-wheat pitas
- 4 ounces hummus
- 6 romaine lettuce leaves
- 2 ounces tomatoes, chopped
- 2 ounces chopped and pitted Kalamata olives

Directions

1. Heat olive oil in a large frying pan on medium heat

2. Sauté onion, bell pepper, oregano and garlic in the oil for 5 minutes until onions are translucent

3. Place pitas in the microwave and heat for 15 seconds

4. Cut pita in half so you are left with 6 pockets

5. Fill the pockets with even amounts of hummus, onion mixture, lettuce, tomatoes and olives

18. Wonton Taco Cups

Wontons are the perfect size for the bento box and taste delicious. Add lime juice to the avocado so they don't turn brown before your little one eats them.

Preparation time-25 minutes

Servings-8

Ingredients

- 12 ounces lean ground beef
- ½ ounce taco seasoning, low-sodium
- 1 Roma tomato, halved
- 2 mini sweet peppers, halved with seeds and stems removed
- ¼ small sweet onion
- ½ ounce fresh cilantro, chopped
- 2 dozen wonton wrappers
- 4 ounces low-fat Cheddar cheese, shredded
- 2 peeled and pitted avocados, sliced
- 1 juiced lime

Directions

1. Preheat oven to 350 degrees Fahrenheit.

2. Coat a 24-cup mini muffin tin with cooking spray

3. Heat large frying pan on medium. Brown beef in the frying pan for 5-7 minutes until meat is cooked through and crumbly. Break up the larger pieces of beef and drain.

4. Stir in taco seasoning until all the beef is coated.

5. In a blender, process tomato, onion, peppers and cilantro until finely chopped.

6. Transfer tomato mixture to the beef and mix well

7. Arrange wanton wrappers in the muffin cups and evenly divide beef mixture in each. Top with cheese

8. Bake for 12-14 minutes until brown around the edges

9. Pack with avocados tossed in lime juice until ready to eat

19.Cheesy Taco Salad

This recipe is a cheesy and delicious alternative to the regular sandwich lunch you might be used to. Your kids will love digging into this savoury salad.

Preparation time-25 minutes

Servings-8

Ingredients

- 24 ounces cooked medium pasta shells, drained
- 2 ounces chipotle Ranch dressing
- 12 ounces lean ground beef
- 1/3 ounce taco seasoning, low-sodium
- 4 ounces mini sweet pepper rings
- 1 peeled and pitted avocado, chopped
- 8 ounces grape tomatoes, quartered
- 8 ounces Monterrey-Jack cheese, cut in cubes

Directions

1. Combine pasta shells and Ranch dressing in a large mixing bowl

2. Heat frying pan on medium heat and brown beef in the pan for 5-7 minutes until cooked through. Break up large pieces of meat. Drain.

3. Stir in taco seasoning until beef is thoroughly coated.

4. Stir all Ingredients together in a large bowl until mixed well

20. Lunchbox Crepes

Crepes are made from scratch or from a prepared package at the grocery store. I like to make the bananas really cold before packing them so they keep their color.

Preparation time-15 minutes

Servings-2

Ingredients

- 1/2 chopped banana
- 4 ounces chopped strawberries
- 2 ounces plain Greek yogurt
- 1 teaspoon honey
- 2 slices chopped deli sliced ham
- 1 ounce low-fat Cheddar cheese, shredded
- 2 x 7" crepes, halved
- 2 ounces blueberries
- 2 ounces baby carrots
- ½ ounce Ranch dressing

Directions

1. In a mixing bowl, combine bananas, yogurt, strawberries and honey.

2. Add fruit mixture to a small container in the lunch box.

3. Place ham and cheese in another container for easy assembly at lunch.

4. Distribute the crepe halves between the Ingredients and pack with blueberries, carrots and Ranch dressing

21.Turkey Taco Salad

This salad is a great recipe that will use up any leftover turkey taco meat from the night before. Pack this with some crispy fruit from Crispy Green and Iago yogurt drink.

Preparation time-15 minutes

Servings-1

Ingredients

- 8 ounces romaine lettuce, chopped
- 2 ounces leftover turkey taco meat
- 1 ounce Mexican cheese, shredded
- 4 cherry tomatoes, quartered
- 2 ounces single serving mini guacamole cups
- 1 ounce baked tortilla chips

Directions

1. Put tacos together with lettuce, meat, Mexican cheese and tomaotes.

2. Pack in bento box with mini guacamole cups and tortilla chips

22.Mandarin Pasta Salad Bento Box

I would suggest sliced kiwi and steamed edamame as suitable side dishes for this pasta salad. Mandarin oranges also make a refreshing change for this lunch.

Ingredients

- 1 peeled kiwi, sliced
- 4 ounces steamed edamame pods
- Serve with kiwi and edamame

Preparation time-15 minutes

Servings-1

Ingredients

- 16 ounces cooked rotini pasta, drained and rinsed
- 6 sliced mini sweet peppers
- 3 peeled mandarins, separated in segments
- 3 sliced green onions
- 16 ounces chopped baby spinach
- 4 ounces matchstick carrots
- 4 ounces sesame ginger dressing
- 2 ounces Chow Mein noodles

Directions

1. Combine all Ingredients except for Chow Mein noodles in a large mixing bowl and toss until mixed well.

2. Transfer pasta salad to the large container in the bento box and pack Chow Mein noodles in a separate container so they stay crunchy.

23.Fruity Pita Quesadillas

Do you remember your mom making you peanut butter and banana sandwiches for lunch when you were a kid? This quesadilla is a fun take on the same idea. If your school doesn't allow for peanuts, then use soy butter instead.

Preparation time-15 minutes

Servings-4

Ingredients

- 4 whole wheat pitas
- 2 ounces plain cream cheese
- 6 sliced strawberries
- 1 sliced kiwi
- 2 ounces red seedless grapes
- 2 ounces peanut butter

Directions

1. Preheat oven to 350 degrees Fahrenheit

2. Arrange whole-wheat pitas directly on the middle rack of the oven and bake for 5-6 minutes.

3. Remove from heat and cool for 10-15 minutes.

4. Spread plain cream chees on 2 rounds of pita and top with fruit.

5. Spread peanut butter on the other 2 rounds of pita and close into a sandwich.

6. Slice pitas into quarters.

24.Pizza Pasta Salad

Litehouse makes a great Homestyle Ranch Dressing & Dip Single that is the perfect size for single serving bento box lunches. If you don't want this recipe is too spicy then substitute Monterrey Jack cheese for mild marble cheddar.

Preparation time-20 minutes

Servings-8

Ingredients

Pizza Pasta Salad

- 16 ounces cooked rotini pasta, drained and rinsed
- 4 ounces Monterrey jack cheese, cut in cubes
- 3 sliced mini sweet peppers
- 2 ¼ ounce can sliced olives, drained
- 6 ounces tomatoes
- 2 ounces mini pepperoni slices
- 1/4 chopped sweet onion
- 2 ounces light Italian dressing

Sides

- 2 ounces baby carrots
- 1 stalk celery, sliced into 2" pieces
- 1 ½ ounces Ranch Dressing & Dip
- 1 pkg. Crispy Green® freeze-dried fruit

Directions

1. When the pasta is cool combine it with the rest of the salad Ingredients in a large mixing bowl and toss to fully incorporate.

2. Place sides in separate containers for easy access at lunch

25. Wafflewich Bento Box

I just love saying the word 'wafflewich' and the kids always get a kick out of saying it to their friends at school. I have used blueberry waffles in this recipe as well as plain with delicious results.

Preparation time-20 minutes

Servings-8

Ingredients

- 2 multigrain waffles, toasted
- 1/2 ounce light cream cheese
- 1 slice pineapple
- 1/2 small thinly-sliced kiwi
- 1/2 peeled mandarin, separated into segments
- 1/2 hard-boiled egg
- 1 pkg. Crispy Green® freeze-dried fruit

Directions

1. Spread toasted waffles with light cream cheese and top with 1 slice of pineapple and kiwi.

2. Cut the waffle into quarters and arrange in the large area of the bento box. Add side dishes for a complete lunch.

26.Black Bean Empanadas

Wholly Guacamole® makes delicious mini cups that are perfect for packing in bento boxes. This empanada is one of my kids' favourite lunches because it tastes great.

Preparation time-10 minutes

Servings-6

Ingredients

- 1 dozen thawed frozen empanada discs
- 1/2 teaspoon olive oil
- 3 finely chopped mini sweet peppers
- 2 ounces sweet onions, finely chopped
- 4 ounces tomatoes, chopped
- 8 ounces low-sodium black beans, drained and rinsed
- ½ ounce taco seasoning, low-sodium
- 6 ounces low-fat Cheddar cheese, shredded
- 1 large beaten egg white
- 2 ounces single serving guacamole minis
- 1 pkg. Crispy Green® freeze-dried fruit

Directions

1. Heat olive oil in a frying pan on medium heat. Sauté peppers, onions and tomatoes in the oil for 3-4 minutes until softened.

2. Stir in black beans and taco seasoning and cook for 2-3 minutes. Remove from heat and set aside.

3. Preheat oven to 375 degrees Fahrenheit.

4. Line a baking sheet with parchment paper and lay the empanada dough out on the paper.

5. Transfer black bean mixture to the empanada dough and top with ½ ounce of cheese.

6. Fold the empanada and brush with egg wash. Press down on the edges with a fork to crimp.

7. Bake empanada for 20 minutes until golden brown

8. Remove from heat and let cool before packing in the bento box.

9. Send the kids off with guacamole cups and Crispy Green crispy fruit for dessert.

27.Apple Zucchini Mini Muffins

These sweet muffins will surprise and delight your kids when they open their lunchbox. Pack these muffins with some applesauce or yogurt and fresh vegetables like cucumber slices.

Preparation time-15 minutes

Servings-8

Ingredients

- 8 ounces whole-wheat flour
- 1/4 teaspoon salt
- 1/2 teaspoon ground cinnamon
- 1 teaspoon baking soda
- 4 ounces honey
- 1 teaspoon vanilla extract
- 1 ½ ounces plain Greek yogurt
- 1 large egg
- 8 ounces drained zucchini, grated
- 4 ounces Gala apple, grated

Directions

1. Preheat oven to 350 degrees Fahrenheit. Spray 24-tin mini muffin pan with cooking spray and set aside.

2. In a mixing bowl, mix the flour, salt, soda and cinnamon and mix well.

3. In a separate bowl, combine honey, vanilla, egg and yogurt.

4. Stir the flour mixture in to the honey mixture and fold until just combined.

5. Fold grated zucchini and apple into the batter and

6. Mix honey, yogurt, egg and vanilla in separate bowl.

7. Add dry Ingredients to wet Ingredients and mix until just incorporated. Fold in zucchini and apple. Fill cups in muffin pan ¾ of the way up with the batter and bake for 15-17 minutes until a tester inserted in the middle comes out clean.

28.One-Pot Cheeseburger Mac

This delicious mac and cheese recipe uses lean turkey, but I have also used extra-lean ground beef or ground chicken as substitutes in a pinch. My kids like to have a bit of mustard added to a container for this recipe too, but you can omit that.

Preparation time-15 minutes

Servings-6

Ingredients

- ½ ounce olive oil
- 16 ounces lean ground turkey
- 1 small finely chopped sweet onion
- 8 ounces chopped mini sweet peppers
- 1 tsp sugar
- 1½ tsp paprika
- 1/2 tsp chili powder
- 1 /2 tsp salt
- 12 ounces water
- 8 ounces milk
- 1 ½ ounces tomato paste
- 12 ounces whole grain dry macaroni
- 8 ounces Cheddar cheese, shredded

Directions

1. Heat oil in a large frying pan on medium high. Sauté turkey, peppers and onion in the oil for 7-10 minutes until turkey is no longer pink inside

2. In a mixing bowl, combine sugar, paprika, chili powder and salt. Pour paprika mixture into the turkey and stir until meat is coated.

3. Bring mixture in the frying pan to a boil. Reduce heat and simmer for 10-12 minutes until pasta is al dente and liquid has been absorbed.

4. Remove mixture from heat and sprinkle with cheese to taste.

29.Fruity Peanut Butter and Jelly

If the school doesn't allow for peanut butter, then soy butter will work well in this recipe as a substitute. Litehouse makes a great single serving cup of Blue Cheese Dressing and Dip that you can pack easily in the bento box.

Preparation time-15 minutes

Servings-1

Ingredients

- 2 slices whole-wheat bread
- 1 ounce peanut butter
- ½ peeled kiwi, thinly sliced
- 1 strawberry thinly sliced
- 4 ounces baby carrots
- 4 ounces popcorn
- 1 mandarin
- 1 ½ ounces blue cheese dressing and dip

Directions

1. Spread peanut butter on one side of each slice of whole-wheat bread

2. Place strawberry and kiwi on the peanut butter, close the sandwich and cut in half.

3. Add baby carrots, mandarin segments, popcorn and blue cheese dip to the other containers in the bento box

30.Stuffed Mini Pepper Boats

If you have an extendable bento box that gives you enough height for the sails on the peppers, then this recipe will delight and amaze your kids for lunch. I use mini-skewers when I am out of coffee stirrers and they work just as well.

Preparation time-15 minutes

Servings-4

Ingredients

- 1/2 ripe peeled and pitted avocado, mashed
- 5 ounces solid white albacore tuna packed in water
- 1/2 chopped stalk celery
- 1 ounce red onion, chopped
- 1/3 ounce lemon juice
- 1/8 teaspoon salt
- 1/8 teaspoon pepper
- 6 mini sweet peppers, cut in half along the length
- 1 peeled mandarin, segmented
- 6 coffee stirrers, halved

Directions

1. Combine avocado, celery, tuna, red onion and lemon juice in a bowl and mix thoroughly

2. Stuff peppers with the tuna mixture. Add a segment of clementine to the skewer and make a sale for the pepper boat.

Conclusion

Whether your child is in daycare, elementary school or navigating their way through high school, the bento box is the perfect container to store their nutritious lunch for the day. These boxes will hold several containers and have enough space and compartments to pack an item from each major food group and still room for a treat or two. I would definitely recommend getting a bento box for your kids' lunch.

About the Author

A native of Albuquerque, New Mexico, Sophia Freeman found her calling in the culinary arts when she enrolled at the Sante Fe School of Cooking. Freeman decided to take a year after graduation and travel around Europe, sampling the cuisine from small bistros and family owned restaurants from Italy to Portugal. Her bubbly personality and inquisitive nature made her popular with the locals in the villages and when she finished her trip and came home, she had made friends for life in the places she had visited. She also came home with a deeper understanding of European cuisine.

Freeman went to work at one of Albuquerque's 5-star restaurants as a sous-chef and soon worked her way up to head chef. The restaurant began to feature Freeman's original dishes as specials on the menu and soon after, she began to write e-books with her recipes. Sophia's dishes mix local flavours with European inspiration making them irresistible to the diners in her restaurant and the online community.

Freeman's experience in Europe didn't just teach her new ways of cooking, but also unique methods of presentation. Using rich sauces, crisp vegetables and meat cooked to perfection, she creates a stunning display as well as a delectable dish. She has won many local awards for her cuisine and she continues to delight her diners with her culinary masterpieces.

Author's Afterthoughts

I want to convey my big thanks to all of my readers who have taken the time to read my book. Readers like you make my work so rewarding and I cherish each and every one of you.

Grateful cannot describe how I feel when I know that someone has chosen my work over all of the choices available online. I hope you enjoyed the book as much as I enjoyed writing it.

Feedback from my readers is how I grow and learn as a chef and an author. Please take the time to let me know your thoughts by leaving a review on Amazon so I and your fellow readers can learn from your experience.

My deepest thanks,

Sophia Freeman

Subscribe to the Newsletter!

https://sophia.subscribemenow.com/

Printed in Great Britain
by Amazon